POTTERY
TECHNIQUES
OF
NATIVE
NORTH AMERICA

POTTERY TECHNIQUES OF NATIVE NORTH AMERICA

An Introduction to Traditional Technology

JOHN KENNARDH WHITE

Photographs by Stewart J. MacLeod

The University of Chicago Press
Chicago and London

Library of Congress Cataloging in Publication Data
White, John Kennardh.
   Pottery techniques of native North America.
   (A University of Chicago Press Text/Fiche)
   1. Pottery craft.   2. Indian craft.   3. Indians of North America-Pottery.
4. Cherokee Indians-Pottery.   I. Title.
TT920.W47   738.1   76-10710
ISBN 0-226-69815-7

The University of Chicago Press, Chicago 60637
The University of Chicago Press, Ltd., London
© 1976 by John Kennardh White
All rights reserved. No part of this publication may be reproduced or transmitted in any form or by any means, electronic or mechanical, including photocopy, recording, or any information storage or retrieval system now known or to be invented, without permission in writing from the publisher.
Printed in the United States of America.

CONTENTS

	PAGE NUMBER	FICHE AND FRAME NUMBER
Introduction	1	
Survey of Selected Examples of Pottery from the Southeast	7	1A2-1C11
Tools and Techniques	11	1C12-1F3
A Simple Bowl	15	1F4-1G12
A Bird Effigy Bowl	19	2A1-2C3
An Incised Bowl with Handles	23	2C4-2F7
A Globular Pot with Incised Rim	27	2F8-3D2
A Large Complicated Stamped Pot	33	3D3-4A6
A Large Cord-Marked Pot	39	4A7-4D10
A Long-Necked Bottle	43	4D11-4G12
A Brief Description of Traditional Firing Techniques	47	
Bibliography	51	

DEDICATED TO ARNE BJØRN

Who has devoted his life to the enrichment of the lives of others. His pursuit of this task has taken many forms. During World War II he risked his life to smuggle many Jews out of occupied Denmark. More recently he has devoted his time and energy to the ceramic technology research aspect of the Archaeological Research Center at Lejre, Denmark. Through his many experiments with reconstructing and firing the kilns used by the Bronze and Iron Age potters of Northern Europe, their accomplishments are better appreciated by archaeologists and laymen alike. It is to Arne Bjørn that I owe a realization of the true value of the traditions to which I am heir.

INTRODUCTION

The transmutation of clay from its amorphous state into a stonelike material captures the interest of all who observe the process. The glowing clay, translucent amid the flames, is a sight never forgotten. It is a scene that has been repeated countless times in the thousands of years since man began to make pottery. Ceramics and the technologies required to produce them are of interest to many different people. To the archaeologist studying potteryproducing cultures pot sherds have often been the primary source of insight into the dynamics of the lifeways of a long vanished people. To modern-day craftsworkers the ceramics of other times and places can provide a source of inspiration and insight that can benefit their own work. To those who are the descendants of cultures possessing strong pottery traditions the serious study of surviving works can revitalize cultural expressions long silent. This work is an attempt to speak to those in each one of these categories and to anyone else who might be interested.

While the total range of shapes and modes of decoration of pottery found in North America is quite large, there are many shared traits. Utilizing a small sample of pottery, largely from the Southeast, I will attempt to duplicate original pieces. The technology involved in this experiment will be more or less that of the traditional Cherokee potter, as I was instructed in it and as I observed it. This is not to say these pots were originally manufactured in the same manner as I will attempt to duplicate them. The methods used to solve various problems, of increasing complexity, may be of some benefit to those concerned with ceramic technology. It may help to supply possible explanations of puzzling features of some pottery types. Hopefully, this work will enable those interested in duplicating these or similar wares to be able to do so.

There have been numerous attempts to revive the making of traditional pottery in many Native American communities. Unfortunately, these have never resulted in the creation of pottery that closely resembled the work of the old potters. I feel that this lack of success is due to two main factors. The technique and approach toward the craft has been that of the modern twentieth-century art school, which is a very different cultural scene. In addition, fine examples of pottery from the traditions supposedly being revived are not used as a gauge against which to measure technical progress. The only traditional ceramic technology in North America that has survived to the present time, outside of the Southwest, is that of the Cherokee. The techniques demonstrated and described later should be considered a core of methods and concepts that can be modified and expanded to deal with specific problems in traditional ceramics.

My interest and involvement with the art of traditional ceramics has continued, with dormant spells every now and then, since my childhood. I inherited several heirloom pottery paddles as well as other tools and pieces of old pottery from my great aunt. Sally Hicks belonged to the Anigilohi Clan of the Cherokee people known as the Chickamauga Band. She belonged to the lineage of The Dragging Canoe, the principal war leader of the Cherokee during the American Revolutionary War. My father, Joseph White, was born in the Sequatchie Valley not far from the Tennessee River, in the heart of the old Chickamauga territory.

My father took me as a child to visit practicing craftsworkers of the Eastern Band of Cherokee in the late 1940's. I remember trying to track down the sites of some of the famous old Cherokee towns, looking for the old townhouse mounds. We spent many a day walking the plowed fields picking up arrowheads and fragments of pottery. The pieces of pottery often bore the impressions of a carved wooden paddle, like those I received from my great aunt. Sometimes the pottery bore the impressions of cords. Aunt Sally had said once that if you did not have a carved paddle, you could wrap string around a stick and use that.

In the 1950's, as I was walking along a hillside near Osan, Korea, something happened to catch my eye, a grey something in the red-clay soil. When I bent down to pick it up, I saw that it was a piece of grey pottery. The surface was covered by a network of lines at right angles to each other. The pot had been decorated by a wooden paddle carved with a checked pattern of grooves. In my mind I saw similar pieces of pottery with similar checked patterns, found in the red clay of north Georgia. I recalled hearing an elderly Cherokee woman saying, "If someone couldn't carve a fancy design, they could just carve a paddle into a lot of little squares—it would work just as good!" I felt a sense of kinship with that small sherd.

After I returned to the States and civilian life, I was eventually drawn to art school to study ceramics formally. I spent some six years studying within this new tradition. I then became involved in native American cultural transmission as a field of academic study. In 1972 I went to Europe to study environmental approaches to teaching about a culture, utilizing a travel grant from the Stone Foundation. My purpose in going there was to study a reconstructed Iron Age village and assess its applicability in creating other environments within which to learn a traditional culture. While at the Historic/Archaeological Research Center near Lejre, Denmark, I had the great honor to work with Arne Bjørn, the European expert on pottery kilns and firing techniques of the Neolithic, Bronze, and Iron Age.

I had brought my ancient heirloom pottery paddle with me, intending to demonstrate Cherokee techniques. I saw this as part of a two-way cultural enrichment exercise. I must admit that it was Arne Bjørn who taught me what a precious thing I had fallen heir to. The modern Danes had to grope back through long periods of time to search for their roots. I suddenly realized that *I* was part of an unbroken line of potters that stretched far back into the past. Generations of potters had kept this wonderful tradition alive; now it seemed for the first time I realized that it was my turn.

In 1975 I spent nine months demonstrating traditional pottery techniques one day a week in the exhibit halls of the Field Museum. This project, funded by the Illinois Arts Council, enabled me to explore in depth for the first time those techniques I had been initially exposed to in my childhood. Nothing can replace practice when it comes to learning a manual skill. It was the continual practice that led me to realize how basically sound the traditional manufacturing techniques were.

This Text/Fiche edition of pottery techniques of Native North America is an experiment. It is an attempt to use a combination of the written word and color photographic images to pass on a traditional approach to the art of the potter. It is an attempt to utilize a traditional means of cultural transmission in an alien mode. I hope that the synthesis will succeed in communicating something of value to you.

To those Native Americans who may seek to use this work as a teaching aid in the rediscovery of their own traditions I will pass on advice that my father gave to me. Call on the old craftsworkers to help guide your hands. The reports of archaeologists working at sites occupied by your tribe are often invaluable for examples of old pottery. State museums usually have representative collections that can be studied and photographed and are likely to respond to requests for assistance.

To those whose ancestors came from across the seas and who have an interest in the traditions whose roots are so deep in this land: I hope that this approach will enable you to empathize more with our native culture as well as develop your skill in working with clay. Perhaps it will help to kindle an interest in the traditions of your own ancestors. The chances are that somewhere along the line they made fine pottery, too.

And to archaeologists, whatever their origin: I hope that this work will help to breathe some life into those countless sherds you may have been tabulating. Remember that those ancient potters did not make their wares for the purpose of furnishing you with frequency distributions. By involving yourself in the process of duplicating the wares, you may find that those pot sherds will take on a very different meaning. Through the study of artifacts and the skills required to create them we can hopefully gain some added understanding of and empathy for the ways of our ancestors.

The traditional means by which the potter's craft was communicated was to observe continually the work being done and then practice yourself. The order of the images is a sequence of actions, from the lump of clay to the finished pot. The images are designed to be looked at in sequence in order to understand fully what is going on. The different pots to be copied increase in size and complexity, and each has a different set of problems to solve. The selection of pots is not definitive; there are many types that are not represented. Perhaps the most glaring absence is that of the slip-decorated traditions. There is not room in this work to cover these wares—perhaps at another time.

The technique of photographing pottery is difficult, but to photograph a potter at work is almost impossible. My friend Stewart MacLeod survived this project and we are still on speaking terms. His continual flow of energy and enthusiasm enabled the project to be completed.

Original pottery from the collections of the Field Museum of Natural History are identified by a catalog number and the prefix FMNH.

SURVEY OF SELECTED EXAMPLES
OF POTTERY FROM THE SOUTHEAST

1A1	*Pottery Techniques of Native North America*
1A2	FMNH # 59994. Bowl with incised design above shoulder. Walton Co., Fla.
1A3	FMNH # 50364. Bowl with incised design above shoulder; two handles. Ala.
1A4	FMNH # 59996. Bowl with elaborate impressed design; ogee repeat on neck and interlocking wave design on shoulder. Walton Co., Fla.
1A5	FMNH # 50382. Elaborately engraved pot with strap and lug handles; overall pattern resembling fish scales. St. Francis Co., Ark.
1A6	FMNH # 50434. Bowl with incised design around shoulder with ribbing between shoulder and rim. Cross Co., Ark.
1A7	FMNH # 50392. Bowl with incised design around neck and strap handles. St. Francis Co., Ark.
1A8	FMNH # 50360. Bowl with incised design around neck and overall pattern of excised spots. St. Francis Co., Ark.
1A9	FMNH # 50418. Bowl with ribs between shoulder and neck. Cross Co., Ark.
1A10	FMNH # 7949. Bowl with multiple handles and rows of excised spots around shoulder. Chickasawba Mound, Mississippi Co., Ark.
1A11	FMNH # 50524. Bowl with handles modified to resemble a fish. Poinsett Co., Ark.
1A12	FMNH # 7987. Small bowl with notched rim, multiple strap handles and overall pattern of excised spots on body. Chickasawba Mound, Mississippi Co., Ark.
1B1	FMNH # 50727. Small bowl with four strap handles and overall pinched pattern. Cross Co., Ark.
1B2	Uncataloged # 766636. Oval bowl with two handles, elab-

orate incised and impressed design around shoulder. St. Francis Co., Ark.

1B3   FMNH # 50339. Bowl with spout. St. Francis Co., Ark.

1B4   FMNH # 50551. Globular bowl with incised design around neck. Poinsett Co., Ark.

1B5   FMNH # 50377. Bowl with carinated rim with incised design. Seven Mile Island, Ala.

1B6   FMNH # 59984. Bowl with overall pattern of incised lines, zones filled in with excised spots. Walton Co., Fla.

1B7   FMNH # 59983. Bowl with incurved rim, incised linear design with dots. Walton Co., Fla.

1B8   FMNH # 50373. Shallow bowl with vertical rim, incised design on rim. Seven Mile Island, Ala.

1B9   FMNH # 59988. Bowl with notched rim and elaborately incised body. Walton Co., Fla.

1B10 FMNH # 59990. Effigy bowl with elaborate zoned incising on body. Walton Co., Fla.

1B11 FMNH # 59995. Small bowl with incised design. Walton Co., Fla.

1B12 FMNH # 50641. Small cup, flat bottom, vertical sides, incised scroll design. Ala.

1C1   FMNH # 59993. Small bowl with notched rim and incised lines and bumps above shoulder. Walton Co., Fla.

1C2   FMNH # 7938. Effigy bowl, bird. Chickasawba Mound, Mississippi Co., Ark.

1C3   FMNH # 50671. Effigy bowl, dog. Cross Co., Ark.

1C4   FMNH # 50645. Effigy bowl, human. Crittenden Co., Ark.

1C5   FMNH # 50905. Effigy bowl, feline (?). St. Francis Co., Ark.

1C6   FMNH # 50648. Effigy bowl, human. Poinsett Co., Ark.

1C7   FMNH # 50656. Effigy bowl, rare form with two animals standing on lug handles. Cross Co., Ark.

1C8   FMNH # 50626. Effigy bowl with elaborate incising. Bolivar Co., Miss.

1C9   FMNH # 57768. Effigy bottle, human. Crittendon Co., Ark.

1C10   FMNH # 50839. Effigy bottle, human. Cross Co., Ark.

1C11   FMNH # 50816. Effigy bottle, human. Cross Co., Ark.

TOOLS AND TECHNIQUES

1C12   Cord-marked pottery is characteristic of some of the earliest ceramic traditions and continued in use in many areas up to European contact. The commonest manner of application was probably through the use of a cord-wrapped stick.

1D1   The cord markings are impressed into the clay by rolling the stick over the surface.

1D2   The cord marking can be closely or widely spaced, depending on how the cord is wrapped around the stick. One pass with the cord-wrapped stick will result in a pattern of parallel lines, each bearing the impression of the cord.

1D3   If the stick is then rolled across the cord impressions, another pattern is produced.

1D4   The pattern impressed on the surface of the clay now bears a strong resemblance to cloth. The two can be distinguished by comparison.

1D5   Some of the early ceramics in the Southeast have impressions of cloth on the outer surfaces and sometimes on the inner.

1D6   A class of large coarsely made objects usually known as "salt pans" were made by lining a circular or oval depression with cloth. The clay was then pressed into this mold evenly with the hands. After the clay had dried enough to hold its shape, the cloth could be used to lift out the pot for further drying. The clay has a tendency to crack if left to dry in the mold.

1D7   When the cloth is removed from the clay, it will leave a strong impression behind. If an impression is taken from the clay surface, it will result in a copy of the fabric. A wide range of weaving techniques can be studied using fragments of salt pan ware, even though the cloth that was used has long since rotted away.

1D8   By comparing the impressions of the cross-cord-marked clay with those produced by cloth, one can easily tell the two apart, even without taking a cast.

1D9   Another manufacturing technique that sometimes is mistaken for cord marking is the use of a wooden paddle carved with parallel lines.

1D10   While the results strongly resemble each other, the paddle does not produce the even, twisted impression that the cord-wrapped stick does.

1D11   Another technique involves the use of a paddle bearing a carved design. Such paddles were used by the earliest potters in the southern Appalachians and are still used by Cherokee potters today — an unbroken tradition of over 3,000 years. The paddle used here, from the Chickamauga Band of Cherokee, Sequatchie Valley, Tennessee, was used at least as far back as the grandmother of my great aunt. The paddle design, however, is rarely seen as clearly on the pot itself as it is on this pad of clay.

1D12   Often the impressions overlap and the viewer can make out only a jumble of lines. In some of the stamped wares from Florida there is a tendency to put single impressions on a pot for the visual effect of the design as it was originally carved. Sometimes the impression is "cleaned up" with a bone tool to make it even more striking. Usually it is only by taking a rubbing or tracing of the pattern that its origin is clear by virtue of identical outlines.

1E1   By use of the fingers alone uniform impressions can be made, but the end of a rounded stick or blunt awl can also be used. By studying the inner surface of the pot, one can often determine the particular tool used.

1E2   The incised lines so commonly found in North American pottery can be duplicated through the use of bone implements.

1E3   The angle at which the tool is held determines much of the character of the line.

1E4	The shape of the point can be determined by the shape of the groove it has left in the clay.
1E5	A rather round, flat bone tool, held at an oblique angle, could duplicate the shallow impressions found on this sherd.
1E6	On this sherd a narrower rounded implement was used, held at a somewhat sharper angle.
1E7	The deep and narrow lines on this pot were made with a still narrower point held at a still more vertical angle.
1E8	The nicks forming two rows of indentations around this pot can be duplicated by digging out small bits of clay with the rounded end of an awl. Sometimes this type of design is produced by pressing in a blunt-ended object.
1E9	The incredible interlocking spiral design on this Caddoan pot was produced by the careful use of one tool. Although the spacing of the lines was gauged by the eye alone, the spirals on this pot are perfect.
1E10	The handles on this deep pot have been notched to add variety to what otherwise would be a rather plain design. Often the fingers alone are used to produce this kind of effect.
1E11	The overall pattern pricked into the body of this pot can be easily duplicated.
1E12	On this Florida effigy bowl portions of the pattern are filled in with a fine set of dots. This zoning technique produces very striking designs.
1F1	The rim has been notched slightly with what seems to have been the tip of a fine awl.
1F2	At first glance this small pot appears to have been decorated with a large number of pieces of clay applied all over the surface.
1F3	Upon closer examination, however, the raised portions seem to have been squeezed up from the surface.

A SIMPLE BOWL

1F4 Perhaps the easiest pots to duplicate are the small simple bowls often found within the Mississippian pottery traditions of the Southeast. These wares, typically tempered with crushed shell, appeared in the Mississippi Valley around a thousand years ago. These bowls, from Arkansas, are typical of many.

1F5 Because of the size, a small quantity of clay is all that is needed. A lump of clay about the size of an orange is patted into a uniform ball shape. It is important that no large air bubbles or hard lumps are left in the clay.

1F6 With the thumb a hole is pushed down into the ball. About ½ inch of clay should be left at the bottom. The ball is then rotated while the clay is squeezed between the thumb and first finger. It is important to do this evenly and gradually in order to keep the thickness of the walls even.

1F7 After a while the squeezing can move from the sides to the bottom so that the thickness remains uniform throughout. The clay now begins to take on the shape of a small bowl.

1F8 Since the edge of the pot tends to become a bit uneven, it should be squared off and evened with the fingers. The thickness is checked to make sure it is equal on the bottom and sides.

1F9 The thumb of the right hand is used to stretch out the walls of the small pot to conform to the desired final shape. During this stretching, you must be careful not to make the piece too thin.

1F10 Both hands can now be used to correct the curvature of the pot. This will ensure that the pot remains round after it has been worked on. This truing up of the shape should follow each step of the manufacturing process.

1F11 The small bowl we are attempting to duplicate has two tapered lugs on the rim, and so we must add these. A small piece of clay is rolled between the fingers into a rough shape. It is very important that the clay be moist enough, for if it is too dry, the join will tend to crack in drying. It is a good idea to work as quickly as possible to avoid excessive drying. If you are working out of doors, then work in the shade and out of direct sunlight to avoid too rapid drying of the clay. If a multitude of small cracks appear on the surface of the clay, it has gotten too dry. Start again rather than try to wet it.

1F12 The lug is then pressed firmly into the clay rim and the join smeared over with the finger, leaving no trace after you are finished smoothing.

1G1 When you are through, the lug should look like an extension of the rim. You should not be able to tell you created it by the addition of another piece of clay.

1G2 The matching lug on the other side of the rim is now added. You must be careful to use the same size piece of clay so that the two lugs will match. If you make the lugs at the same time, you can cover one with a damp cloth to keep it from drying out.

1G3 After you have checked the size and placement of the lug, it can be smoothed into the surface as the first one was. Make sure it is in the right place before you attach it firmly. It is very easy, for some reason, to apply clay additions such as these handles a little out of line.

1G4 The bowl can now be placed upside down on a cloth and the underside of the handles properly smoothed to the clay sides.

1G5 The clay is drawn up into the side of the pot. The skill with which you blend the clays together will determine the strength of the join and add to the appearance of the final pot.

1G6 After the handles are joined properly, turn the pot right side up and then readjust its shape.

1G7 Now is a good time to compare your handiwork with the original. The rim between the lugs has been indented in some way.

1G8 By examining the rim closely, one can see that a tool has been used to make a series of notches. There are also indications that the rim was then squeezed between the fingers to return it to a round profile.

1G9 By using a simple rounded tool made from bone, you can easily impress a series of rounded notches around the rim's edge.

1G10 This creates a T-shaped profile as the rim is pushed out by the pressure of the tool. This is a natural result of the use of such pressure on still-soft clay. The notches could be carved out of the rim after it became stiff, but it would take longer and would result in a different appearance.

1G11 The rim is now squeezed back into shape with the fingers. This does not obscure the notches, but it does alter their appearance somewhat. Often several different approaches can be used to achieve the same end result.

1G12 The ultimate test, of course, is how similar in appearance and "feeling" the two pots are.

A BIRD EFFIGY BOWL

2A1 A variation of the simple half-round bowl form is this typical effigy bowl. With a simple lug representing the bird's tail and the head and neck applied to the opposite rim, the bowl becomes the bird's body. This basic configuration is also found in wooden bowls. Pottery forms of this type were very popular over a large part of the country, from the Gulf of Mexico up into the Illinois Valley and from eastern Oklahoma to the Carolinas. This example is from Arkansas.

2A2 A slightly larger ball of clay will be needed, since this pot is a little larger than the preceding one. It is hollowed out with the thumb and first finger in the same manner as our first example.

2A3 After the walls have been thinned and evened, there are marks that have been made by the fingers. These should be removed by careful squeezing until the walls are as smooth as possible.

2A4 With the thumb the clay can be spread out to begin the typical bowl form. The thumb should be drawn repeatedly from the center to the rim, turning the pot each time. This will thin the walls further as well as alter the shape.

2A5 In order to stretch the walls still further a freshwater clam shell was used. The curvature of the shells makes it possible to adjust them to many curves in a pot, and they are, therefore, ideal clay-working tools.

2A6 While the shell is fresh, it will have a rather sharp edge, which makes a perfect working surface. After a while this sharp edge will become blunt. The shell can be sharpened, or it can be discarded for a fresh one.

2A7 The shell should not dig into the clay too much. It should stretch the clay as well as scrape off high places; the result should be a smooth surface with fine scrape marks.

2A8 After the bowl has been thinned sufficiently and has the correct curvature, a piece of clay is prepared for the lug.

	This piece will form a half circle that will become the stylized tail on the completed effigy bowl.
2A9	The clay is pressed into the rim of the bowl until it is firmly attached. The inner wall of the bowl rim should be supported while this is being done in order to minimize any distortion of the rim.
2A10	After the lug is attached, the inner surface of the rim is smoothed and the surfaces blended with the fingers. It should appear to be an extension of the rim rather than a piece of clay stuck onto the side of the pot.
2A11	Here is the head from another bird effigy bowl. This example shows in greater detail some of the natural effects that the old potters were able to achieve with a relatively simple and direct manipulation of the clay. The head on the bowl we are copying is smaller and somewhat simpler in design.
2A12	A small piece of clay is molded with the fingers into a rough form the size of the bird head. It is then attached to the pot before the final finishing of the head.
2B1	The neck is attached to the upper portion of the rim with a twisting motion that will secure the clay firmly. Again, it is important that the clay not be too dry or you will risk a poor join that is likely to crack later on.
2B2	The underside of the neck is smoothed downward onto the side of the pot. This should be done carefully so that there is no pocket of air trapped between the two layers of clay.
2B3	On the inner edge of the rim the bird's neck should be smoothed down but not in such a way that it produces a bump. The inside of the bowl should be a continuous smooth surface.
2B4	The bird's neck on the original effigy bowl has a very large bump, which might represent the curved neck of a water bird or something like an Adam's apple. On this example you can see that it was made from an applied piece of clay.

2B5	A small piece of clay is then pressed onto the pot at the corresponding place. Holding it in the fingers and using a twisting motion will ensure that it is firmly attached.
2B6	The fingers should then smooth the edges of the bump in all directions. This will blend it into the side of the pot so that it becomes visually integrated with the rest of the shape.
2B7	The eyes are commonly made of another applied ball of clay that is pressed firmly into the head. On the larger example a depression, probably made with the end of an awl, forms the pupil.
2B8	The clay balls are pressed into the sides of the head and then blended into the rest of the clay. Oftentimes the edge of a bone awl can be used to smooth the eye, if it proves too delicate for your fingers.
2B9	The head should now be set properly on the rim, with the eyes balanced on both sides. It is very easy to mis-gauge the positioning of one or the other and not notice it until much later. While the clay is still relatively soft, it would be easy to scrape off the out-of-position eye and reattach one. Once the clay dries, it is no longer possible.
2B10	The bird's head on our effigy bowl seems to have some sort of a crest. On this particular example it looks almost more like a warrior's scalplock than a bird's crest.
2B11	A short piece of clay roughly similar in size is pressed onto the top of the head.
2B12	A bone tool can be used to smooth the edges of the crest and join it smoothly to the bird's head.
2C1	The bone tool can also be used to make the cut representing the bird's mouth.
2C2	After the groove is completed, the fingers can be used to go over the bird's head smoothing down the surface. This will result in a form that blends in with the whole so that the pot will look as though it was made from one piece of clay rather than a number of pieces stuck together.

2C3 In this picture of the two effigy bowls together notice that the head of the new pot is drooping forward somewhat. This is due to the softness of the clay and can easily be corrected by propping it up with another piece of clay or by waiting until it stiffens up a bit before pushing it back. If the clay becomes too hard, however, it will probably crack if you try to bend it back.

AN INCISED BOWL WITH HANDLES

2C4 This graceful pot from Arkansas is interesting on several counts. While the profiles of the last two pots were a simple hemisphere, this vessel has a much more complicated set of curves.

2C5 In addition to two different types of handles, two lugs and two strap forms, the body of the pot is covered with an incised all-over design faintly resembling fish scales. This pattern of curved lines also sets off the body from the neck, and the handles, too, are utilized as decoration.

2C6 The beginning of this vessel is the same as the last two. A ball of clay is opened with the thumb and first finger and squeezed, while turning, to form a hollow shape.

2C7 The thickness of the walls is judged by the same two fingers; all the while the pot is turned to keep the form even.

2C8 The thumbs can be drawn up from the center toward the rim to help stretch out the walls.

2C9 The rim is then gently drawn inward. Since the lower portion of this vessel expands and then contracts, the shape we are forming must reflect this.

2C10 The rough form we now have consists of an opening smaller than the widest section below it. This will become the "shoulder" of the finished pot.

2C11 A piece of clay is now squeezed with both hands into a longish shape. This is what is sometimes referred to as a coil or "sausage" of clay.

2C12 By revolving the piece of clay while it is being squeezed alternately by the hands, you can stretch it out into a long but fat uniform shape.

2D1 This coil is then applied to the rim of the already formed section and fastened to the inner side of the lower portion. This is to accommodate the smaller diameter that the neck of this vessel exhibits.

2D2 As the coil is being attached to the base, it is squeezed

	between the fingers into a rectangular cross-section. This serves partially to preform that section of wall.
2D3	Here you can plainly see the difference in thickness after the coil has been attached to the base. This should be done in a regular rhythmic movement.
2D4	Where the coil overlaps, the extra length is pinched off.
2D5	The ends are then pushed together by the thumb and first finger of each hand.
2D6	In this case I misjudged the length of the coil and so have to add a small piece of clay to fill the gap. As long as the clay is sufficiently damp, this poses no problem.
2D7	This patch of clay is pushed into the opening and then smoothed over with the fingers. After you are finished, it should be an invisible patch.
2D8	The neck coil is then smoothed into the body of the pot. In this case smooth the outside seam first, so that the coil will be firmly attached.
2D9	The inner edge can then be smoothed. Support the clay so you can use your right hand without deforming the curve.
2D10	After you have finished the outside seam, check the inner join by feeling it with your fingers. The clay should be smooth, with no gaps.
2D11	The neck section of the vessel can now be stretched and thinned.
2D12	This should result in the upper portion of the vessel reaching approximately its final size.
2E1	At this point the handles will be prepared. There are two types each requiring two pieces. It helps to make them at the same time so that they will be the same size. They can be covered with a damp cloth to keep the clay moist.
2E2	The flat strap handles are formed first. They will be made a little oversize so that the excess can be trimmed off later.
2E3	The flat piece of clay is pressed into the side of the pot. It

	must be joined to the rim and the shoulder, so that it forms a bridge between these two places.
2E4	One hand must be on the inside of the vessel to support it while the handle is being pushed into the clay.
2E5	You can also reach down into the pot to support it while the lower edge of the handle is pressed firmly into the clay.
2E6	Both ends of the handle must be joined well to the body of the pot. When one is completed, the other is applied in the same manner.
2E7	Since this is to be a round-bottomed pot, it must be supported. Lacking a section of gourd, I will use a clay ring, though sometimes a pottery bowl might be used as a support. Cherokee potters have traditionally used sections of bottle gourds to support their round-bottomed forms.
2E8	A dry cloth pad is needed to support the bottom of the pot evenly. This will also help keep the soft clay from sticking to the support.
2E9	The round bottom of this pot will enable it to sit upright in a bed of coals.
2E10	Now that the pot is sitting in its support, the lugs can be applied.
2E11	Again, the fingers support the clay that receives the piece being pushed firmly into it.
2E12	A bone tool can now be used to scrape and even up the handles, to smooth all the joins perfectly as well as to eliminate any excess clay provided originally for matching the two handles.
2F1	A bone awl, like this tool, is especially handy to clean out the opening between the strap handle and the wall of the pot. This is an area that cannot be gotten into with the fingers.
2F2	The lugs are then smoothed and evened using the same tool.
2F3	After the handles are complete, the incising is begun.

This particular pattern begins along the rim. A series of half-circles are scratched into the clay all around the rim. Then another row is begun.

2F4 Each half-circle connects with the center of the one above it. In such a way the scalelike design is formed.

2F5 The curved scales move around the bulge of the pot toward the bottom. The result will be an over-all pattern.

2F6 The punctate patterns on the strap handles are now applied. After this is done, the pot is given a final shaping to correct any unevenness that has developed.

2F7 After the incising is complete, the new pot is checked with the old. Afterwards the surface will be smoothed somewhat with the fingers, and the pattern will be more subtle.

A GLOBULAR POT WITH INCISED RIM

2F8 An additional set of problems in ceramic technique can be found in this globular pot from Arkansas. Although it appears much plainer than the last vessel, it is larger and the body of the pot is globular. This will require a somewhat different technique. This type of pot may have been used for storage purposes, perhaps of select seeds for planting. The rim does not provide a very secure grip since it is not curved outward and the smooth body of the pot would be quite slippery if it got greasy; there are no handles.

2F9 A large lump of clay is taken in the hands. If the clay is fairly damp, it is easy to slap smaller pieces of clay into the lump until it is the size required. If the clay is too dry or picks up dried flakes of clay from its storage place, you will probably see cracks developing in your pot as it dries.

2F10 It is important that the clay be patted into a perfectly round shape prior to forming your opening. If the ball is uneven, it will be difficult to keep the walls of the pot a uniform thickness as you proceed.

2F11 With a larger lump of clay it becomes a little more difficult to open the ball. It will take more effort to squeeze the clay between the thumb and the first finger so the rest of the hand should help. Rotate the ball a little at a time to ensure even progress.

2F12 As the wall becomes thinner, it will be easier to squeeze.

2G1 When the hole in the lump of clay is large enough, the piece can be put over your left hand doubled up into a fist. This technique might be called a paddle and anvil technique with the right hand functioning as a paddle and the left fist becoming the anvil.

2G2 The hand is patted firmly on the clay in a motion that will slap the clay several times, moving from the base to the edge. The movement of the fist within is from the knuckles to the wrist.

2G3   Twisting your fist sharply will cause the lump of clay to revolve some. This will enable you to stretch the clay uniformly down your arm, all the while thinning it. With this technique it is easy to tear the clay apart, so you must proceed carefully.

2G4   After the clay is sufficiently stretched, it is placed in a round-bottom support. This will make it easier and more convenient to turn the pot as you work on it. The traditional Cherokee bottle gourd sections are more convenient than this clay ring because they are easier to turn.

2G5   Clam shells can be used to thin and shape the walls of the pot or, as in this case, the fingers of one hand while the other supports the outside.

2G6   While the base is turned, the hands continually thin and shape the soft clay. Attention must be paid to keeping the top edge as even as possible, and doing so will help you to judge the thickness of the wall.

2G7   The hands are now beginning to stretch the walls outward. The upper edge is squeezed in slightly while the fingers of the hand on the inside move from the bottom upward, stretching the clay outward.

2G8   This process will make the pot assume, gradually, a globular shape. Alternate the stretching outward of the walls with a slight squeezing of the rim.

2G9   When the walls are curved out sufficiently, the edge is made even. This will prepare it for the addition of a new coil of clay needed to extend the wall upward.

2G10   A thick coil of soft clay is now pressed into the inner side of the top edge. This is pressed firmly into a square or rectangular cross-section the same thickness as the rest of the pot.

2G11   The end of the coil is squeezed off with the fingers and then joined with the beginning. This should then be smoothed together so that the connection does not show.

2G12   The inner join with the body of the pot cannot be seen; it must be smoothed over with the fingers by feel alone.

3A1   Support the clay with one hand while using the other to smooth the join on the outside. The hand on the inside must keep the inward-curving edge from collapsing.

3A2   After the seam has been completely smoothed over, the contour of the pot should be checked. If it has become uneven, it can be easily corrected now.

3A3   A coil is now added that will become the upraised rim matching the one on the old pot we are attempting to duplicate.

3A4   The coil should join accurately, for a thin spot will be very noticeable on the rim of the finished pot.

3A5   Again, one hand should be supporting the wall on the inside while the coil is being smoothed down onto the body of the pot.

3A6   After the join is complete, the thickness of the upper part of the pot should be again checked. This can be done by feeling the thickness of the clay between your thumb and fingertips.

3A7   The rim is now checked carefully. If there is any uneven spot a small piece of soft clay can be pressed in and smoothed into the surface.

3A8   The fingers should now be used to give the final curve you want the pot to have. Although templates can be used to check the complex curves, you should practice using your eye to judge.

3A9   I am using a clam shell on the inside to correct the curve of the body into a more globular form. If it had been too much distended, I would have used both hands finger-tip to finger-tip to squeeze it gently back into shape.

3A10 I am now examining the original pot to check on the rim incising. The clay should stiffen some before you begin to scratch in the design.

3A11 By examining the design carefully and noting the character of the lines, you can hopefully discover the order in which the potter proceeded with the engraving. This will allow you to understand the underlying principles by which the design was laid out and completed. Note especially where lines overlap one another; you can tell which one was incised first. If the design appears cramped at one point, it may be where the design ended and the potter ran out of space before the last unit of the pattern could be repeated properly.

3A12 Since it appears that the first elements worked into the old pot were the notches around the rim, I will start with them.

3B1 The design is probably derived from a variety of finger-woven sashes or belts. Historic examples made by the Mojave people are known from the Southwest. Ancient sashes bearing the same design have been found preserved in caves in that part of the country.

3B2 The design begins with a triangle filled with parallel lines.

3B3 Then another triangle is formed, and this space filled with a set of parallel lines at right angles to the others.

3B4 In this way the band of triangles progresses around the rim of the pot. As you near the beginning, you should keep an eye on spacing.

3B5 After the row of incised triangles is complete, several rows of spots will finish the design.

3B6 After completing the pattern, I realize that the shoulder of the new pot curves gradually into the rim and the design is much wider than that of the original. The S-shape of the recurved contours of traditional pots looks simple but is extremely subtle.

3B7 By comparing the new with the old, I can see that by not developing a correct angle to the rim, perspective was lost. While the clay is still soft enough, I can take one of the bone tools and smooth out the incised lines. If the clay is too dry or the lines too deep this would not be possible.

3B8 To make sure, I begin incising the pattern again using the old pot as a guide.

3B9 By following the original closely, I am now able to

duplicate the design much better.

3B10 I have decided to use another bone tool to make the spots around the bottom of the triangles in order to duplicate the original more closely.

3B11 After the engraving is completed, the pot can be turned over on the rim. It should be stiff enough by now to hold its shape, but if the pot begins to slump at all, quickly put it back on the support. There will be uneven places where the soft clay adjusts to the support or folds in the cloth.

3B12 Soft clay is pushed into the depressions caused by the edge of the support.

3C1 Quite large depressions can be patched in this manner. If the clay is too dry, it can be dampened slightly. But cover it with a damp cloth rather than drip water on it.

3C2 Note that the pattern of the cloth is strongly impressed on the bottom of this pot. Frequently pottery that has been decorated in another manner will show a pattern of cloth on the base. If only a few broken sherds of the base of such a pot were found, it would be logical to assume it was from a fabric-marked pot.

3C3 A clam shell is now used to scrape the outside of the vessel to produce a smooth and even surface.

3C4 The clam shell scrapes over the surface removing the high spots. The sharp edge of the shell should ride over the surface shaving off the irregularities.

3C5 By changing the angle at which the shell is held, you can draw it along, compressing the clay. This has to be done after the bumps have been removed, or it will accentuate them.

3C6 Here you can see a portion of the pot that has been scraped and smoothed.

3C7 The clam shell can also be used to scrape the inside of the vessel. It must be small enough that the full curve of the clam shell can touch the clay surface. Otherwise the ends of the shell will tend to gouge grooves and result in a very rough inner surface.

3C8   After the clam shell has been drawn along the inner surface from the base toward the rim, the clay shavings should be lifted out.

3C9   The clay can be scraped off the insides of the shoulder more conveniently if the pot can rest on its side. The support should be well padded with cloth so it doesn't mar the finish on the outside.

3C10 The shell is now being used to thin the neck of the vessel by careful scraping. As this action scrapes some of the tempering material out of the clay it leaves a distinctive surface. Once you have seen it, the result is easy to notice, even on a small fragment.

3C11 A smooth pebble is now being used to polish the outer surface of the pot. The clay must be damp enough to produce a sheen when the pebble compacts the surface.

3C12 The pebble compacting the surface will cause the clay on the surface actually to flow. If you go over any of the incised lines, they will be partially obscured.

3D1   The lines can then be gone over with a fine awl if you want to make them sharp and distinct again.

3D2   One of the rewards of developing skill is the satisfaction of seeing the results of your labor!

A LARGE COMPLICATED STAMPED POT

3D3   The large pot here illustrated is an example of the complicated stamp tradition. This particular piece (FMNH # 49647) was found in southeast Georgia.

3D4   Because the pattern impressed in the clay was difficult to see, a little powdered chalk has been rubbed across the surface to make the design show up more readily. Note that the overlapping paddle impressions make it very difficult to discern the complete design.

3D5   Utilizing the traditional Cherokee technique for making a large paddled pot, a large ball of clay is patted into a flat circular pancake.

3D6   This pad of clay is then thrown onto the bottom of an upturned pot which will become the form over which the bottom of the new vessel will be shaped.

3D7   The right hand is now patted firmly against the soft clay, always moving from the base toward the rim.

3D8   Turn the pot slightly and then repeat this motion. The result should be the gradual stretching of the clay down over the surface of the form.

3D9   When the clay has been stretched evenly, the wooden paddle is used. The paddle must be dipped in water to prevent the clay from sticking to it.

3D10   As when using the hands, the paddle should be applied from what will be the bottom of the finished pot toward the rim. This will continue to stretch the clay, so you must use caution. The usual problem in hand-building pottery seems to be making the walls too thick but with this technique the problem is making them too thin!

3D11   Here you can clearly see the difference between the design as it was carved on the paddle and as it appears in overstamped form on the clay surface. The picture also shows the curvature of the base, one of the main reasons for the development of this technique.

3D12   The partially formed pot is left on its form until the clay loses enough moisture to hold its shape. It is then gently lifted from the pot to keep it from sticking, which might result in a crack.

3E1 When the clay feels strong enough that you can lift it up in this manner, you can transfer it to a curved base. Do *not* attempt to lift it up and turn it over by hand. It will collapse when the weight begins to fall on one rim.

3E2 Instead place the rounded base with its pad of cloth against the pointed bottom and holding them tightly together turn all of them right side up.

3E3 If the pot used as a form seems to be sticking, it can be twisted slightly, to break any suction that might be causing the problem.

3E4 The pot is then slowly lifted up out of the fresh clay. Lifting it straight up will not distort the still somewhat soft clay. The pad of cloth should protect the rounded or conoidal bottom of the pot you are to make. It is extremely difficult to do this without having fairly thick walls to support the outward slope of the clay.

3E5 A coil of clay is now utilized to begin the raising of the walls.

3E6 If the clay is squeezed to the thickness of the already formed walls, less strain will be felt and a more even surface will result.

3E7 As the top edge of the base was a bit uneven, I am finishing this coil off after one circuit.

3E8 The flattened coil is carefully smoothed into the textured surface, and its upper edge is made even.

3E9 When this has been done another coil is prepared that will increase the height and decrease the diameter as well.

3E10 The ability to squeeze out even rolls of clay quickly is a prerequisite to satisfactory hand-building of pottery.

3E11 The end of the coil of clay is smoothed into the wall by tapering and then pressing and smoothing. As the coil is

	carried around, it will cross over the end thus becoming a spiral.
3E12	The clay coil can also be given some curvature while it is squeezed into the right thickness. When the curve of the pot is moving inward the coil should be pressed into the inner edge of the section already formed. If the curvature is in the opposite direction and the pot is becoming larger, then press the new coil onto the outer edge of the wall.
3F1	As always the coils should be smoothed into the previous section as soon as they have been pressed together.
3F2	As soon as several circuits of new wall have been finished you can focus your attention on finishing the outer surface.
3F3	Using a round stone as a support for the inside of the new pot, I am using the paddle to impress the design over the new section of wall.
3F4	By striking the wet paddle so as to push the clay against the upper surface of the stone, I can maintain the inward curve of the wall.
3F5	Sometimes there will be suction develop between the clay and the stone. This can be broken by giving the stone a slight twist.
3F6	If the twisting of the stone occurs at the same time the wooden paddle is taken away, the action should not distort the clay.
3F7	The paddling process should completely cover the outer surface of the pot. As the moisture will have softened the clay, it is usually advisable to let the pot rest and dry out slightly.
3F8	If there is any distortion, it can usually be corrected by cradling the outer surface of the pot in both hands and gently shaping it.
3F9	If the form needs to be expanded this can be easily done by stretching the wall from the inside, using the clam shell.

3F10   Note that in this picture, although a clam shell has been used to go over most of the interior, you can still see the impression of the outer surface of the pot that was originally used as a support or form. Any archaeological ceramics that reveal interior impressions of this nature were probably made utilizing this technique.

3F11   Another coil of clay is added to the pot. Since it is nearing the final height, this coil will make only one circuit.

3F12   This coil is very carefully joined to the previous section of wall.

3G1   The major problem at this stage of the construction is that the walls of the pot will collapse. Thus the new section of wall must be carefully supported on the inside as it is squeezed thinner and smoothed into the rest of the clay.

3G2   As long as the clay is properly supported, there is no great problem.

3G3   When the paddle is being used to finish off this final section of wall, extra care must be used. The walls will shake and quiver fearfully.

3G4   As long as you are careful and twist the stone to break the suction, it should hold its shape without collapsing.

3G5   After you have finished using the paddle and have let the pot sit a while to dry somewhat, you can again use the clam shell to smooth out the impressions on the inside.

3G6   You can also use your fingers to gently squeeze the clay into the proper curve. If you are careful, you will not destroy the pattern. If it smears too easily the clay is too damp; let it dry for a while longer.

3G7   A fine, thin coil is now prepared. This will form the rim and will be applied *over* the paddle-impressed surface of the pot.

3G8   The coil is pressed firmly against the pot. My thumb is on the inside and my other fingers are squeezing both the coil and the paddled surface together.

3G9   This results in reducing the thickness of the two pieces of clay to about the same thickness as the clay wall below it.

3G10   I make another circuit of the rim squeezing and smoothing the upper edge. You should not be able to tell there is a seam there.

3G11   Now the curvature of the rim can be finalized. Continually turn the pot in its base and check to see that it is symmetrical. If a certain place looks as though it is a little flat, the clam shell can be used to ease it back out. You must be extremely gentle, however, because the clay becomes more brittle as it dries and is very easy to crack.

3G12   I am now using a bone awl to make a series of notches along the lower edge of the applied rim coil.

4A1   After the notches are completed, I go over them with my fingers squeezing them. this greatly softens the effect. This notching of the rim coil is a characteristic of Cherokee pottery as it was made in the 1700's; individual potters, however, created the effect in many different ways.

4A2   I just noticed a dent in the inner surface of the pot. I was probably careless with the clam shell and gouged a chunk out of the wall.

4A3   As the clay is rather stiff now, I moisten a small ball of clay with some saliva and press it into the cavity.

4A4   After it dries for a few minutes and absorbs the moisture, the small clay patch will be smeared over the inner surface so that no trace of the addition will remain.

4A5   After a final check on the curves and other nicks, the pot can be left to dry. Drying is best accomplished slowly. If you are working outside, let your pots dry in the shade because if they dry too fast in the sun, they will probably crack or warp badly. If the pot is turned upside down on a piece of cloth, it will dry more slowly because moisture can evaporate only from the outside instead of both the inside and outside. By setting the pot upside down, you will also prevent warping of the rim.

4A6   Here are a few fragments of pottery from a Cherokee town that was destroyed by the Americans in 1776. I guess you could call this a bicentennial pot.

A LARGE CORD-MARKED POT

4A7 The large cord-marked pot illustrated here, although found in Illinois, is typical of the earliest Woodland pottery found in many parts of Eastern North America. This example (FMNH # 207904) clearly shows the pattern of cord impressions radiating from the conical base up toward the rim. I will use basically the same technique utilized in the manufacture of the complicated stamped Cherokee pot. In place of the carved wooden paddle a cord-wrapped stick is used.

4A8 A large pancake of clay is slapped down on a cord-marked pot that has been set on its rim.

4A9 With the thumbs the clay is drawn down from the top, stretching and thinning itself in the process. When it is uniformly expanded in this manner, the cord-marked stick is used.

4A10 The stick is rolled downward, always from the point of what will become the bottom of the new pot. This will also squeeze the clay as it rolls along, thinning it still further. If an unevenness becomes evident, the roller can be used in other directions, this will tend to fill in the low spot.

4A11 When you have used the roller over the entire surface, the places where you smoothed in low spaces will show a characteristic pattern of crossed cord-markings.

4A12 If you look at the bottom of the pot, you will see the cord marks radiate outward from the center of the base. This effect, the natural result of this method, would be very difficult to achieve in another manner.

4B1 As with the Cherokee pot, after the clay has hardened somewhat, it is slipped off the pot and into a supportive base that will preserve the conical bottom. This should also be protected with a folded cloth pad.

4B2 The walls are then coiled up from the cord-marked base. In this case the coil is spiraling around rather than being used to make one circuit at a time.

4B3	The inside coil seams can be smoothed in this manner with the other hand supporting the clay on the outside.
4B4	After the outside coils are also smoothed, the cord-wrapped stick roller is used. In this picture you can clearly see that the roller is squeezing the wall up higher.
4B5	After all the new work is cord marked, the hands are used to even the curve and to contract the upper part of the wall.
4B6	The coiling process then continues. Since the cord-wrapped stick, unlike the wooden paddle does not need to be wet, work can proceed at a quicker pace.
4B7	Here you can see how one downward movement of the thumb is smoothly joining the new coil. This will only work this way if you have already squeezed the coils together so they are the same thickness.
4B8	The clam shells are now used to smooth and stretch the clay on the inside. The numerous depressions made by the fingers can easily be smoothed over in this manner.
4B9	The shell will also be used to increase the curvature of the pot. The other hand is acting as a support to keep control of how much stretching will go on.
4B10	Here I am starting down quite low and increasing the bulge or "belly" of the pot.
4B11	After the work with the clam shell is completed, another coiling process begins.
4B12	When this coil is joined, you must be careful to keep it constricted.
4C1	The inner seam is smoothed together by using the thumb while the other fingers are utilized to control the curvature.
4C2	In this manner the clay can resist the tendency to stretch outward before you want it to.
4C3	The roller is now used again. Note how it stretches the clay upward and outward as well.

4C4   If a place is bulging out slightly the roller can be easily used to push it back into place.

4C5   By increasing the pressure between the roller and the fingers on the inside of the pot, you can reduce extra thickness.

4C6   The use of the roller provides a great deal of control as well as a pleasant surface that will be attractive and less prone to slip out of the hands.

4C7   The clam shells are used once again to remove the various marks left on the inner surface of the pot.

4C8   The final coil is added, and the pot is just about at the right height. At this stage extreme caution must be used or the walls of the pot, still soft, will split irreparably.

4C9   Because the rim will be curved slightly outward, this coil is sitting directly on top of the one beneath it.

4C10 The clay is very carefully smoothed downward to join with the already cord-marked surface below it.

4C11 The roller is now used to thin and mark this last coil of clay.

4C12 Section by section you will work around the rim of the pot. With such a large piece it is easier and safer to shuffle around it as you work, keeping the place you are finishing directly in front of you.

4D1   After the rim section has been completely impressed, the clam shell is again used.

4D2   Places where the surface is irregular can be evened out through the use of the roller with the hand on the inside. If you want to keep all the lines parallel and pointing toward the rim, you can go over it again with the roller.

4D3   The hands are used largely to increase the outward curve of the rim. This should be done gradually, for if you press too rigorously, the walls may develop a split.

4D4   Here again the shell is used to smooth the inside and increase the curvature of the rim.

4D5   As the pot nears completion, you should check it frequently from various perspectives.

4D6   This will help you discover barely noticeable dents or flat areas.

4D7   The upper surface of the rim should be smoothed. A bit of wet leather of a soft variety such as chamois can be folded over the rim and drawn around to smooth it. In some cases this technique can produce surface markings difficult to distinguish from the marks of a potter's wheel.

4D8   The curvature of the rim is now adjusted for the last time.

4D9   In the process I nicked the edge of the rim and have to repair it with a little bit of clay.

4D10 And here is the completed pot, a fair re-creation of one of the oldest types of pottery in North America.

A LONG-NECKED BOTTLE

4D11 The last traditional pot chosen for replication will be a typical Mississipian water bottle. These graceful long-necked forms are commonly found in a buff clay body with a red slip design painted decoration. They appeared in North America around a thousand years ago of Meso-American derivation. This particular example (FMNH # 50435) is from Arkansas. The coloration is due to the firing conditions to which the bottle was subjected, the grey from carbon that penetrated the pores of the clay.

4D12 A lump of clay suitable for making the body of the bottle is made into a ball, which is then flattened with the fist.

4E1 This is then patted over a fist to draw down the clay. This should result in a bowl-like shape.

4E2 With rapid slapping motions the clay is quickly thinned and elongated.

4E3 When the bowl has gotten deep enough, it should be checked for overly thin places on the bottom that should be filled in with clay and smoothed over.

4E4 When the bowl form has perfectly even walls, it should be set into a base.

4E5 The upper edge can now be carefully squeezed in with the hands.

4E6 The fingers can be used to stretch out the sides to make the shape more globular.

4E7 A coil of soft clay is added to close the mouth still further. Once the neck of the bottle is put on, it will be impossible to adjust the inside, so all work must be done carefully.

4E8 The upper surface of the pot is now almost horizontal and very prone to falling in. If the clay is too damp to hold itself, let it dry for a few minutes.

4E9 The aim is to leave only a small hole in the center of a round ball.

4E10	With the final pieces of clay well smoothed there should be no sign of the manner in which it was constructed.
4E11	The bottle is now ready to receive its neck.
4E12	Examining the original, we can see that there is a sort of ring of clay circling the bottom of the neck.
4F1	A small piece of clay is shaped into a ring with a flange.
4F2	The inside of this flange is carefully smoothed with the fingers.
4F3	Finally, the clay is pressed onto the surface of the globular-shaped form.
4F4	With a bent finger to reach down inside, the clay flange is firmly smoothed to the body.
4F5	A piece of clay to become the neck of the bottle is now measured and preshaped.
4F6	With the first finger of the right hand, a channel is pushed gently all the way through this piece of clay.
4F7	When this is smooth and concentric, the finger is slowly pulled out. The neck will become lopsided if care is not used.
4F8	This thick neck is then carefully placed atop the flange.
4F9	With the first finger inside, the other hand smooths and presses the clay until a good tight fit results.
4F10	At this time a round stick is pushed down the neck into the body of the bottle.
4F11	While it is twisted around the neck is squeezed with the other hand.
4F12	Leaving the stick in the neck as a support, you use a bone tool to trim off the excess.
4G1	The stick can now be used to tap the clay gently around the neck to make it uniformly round.
4G2	One of the bone tools is used to trim up the collar at the base of the neck.

4G3	The flat bone awl can also be used to smooth the sides of the neck to remove the marks left by the stick.
4G4	With the stick on the inside of the neck, the bone awl can itself squeeze out irregularities.
4G5	The original is now closely checked and compared with the replica.
4G6	The original has a slight lip at the end of the neck so the neck of the replica is altered to match it.
4G7	After the bottle has dried a while, the clam shell is used to smooth down and shave off irregularities still more.
4G8	A bone tool is used to make the indentation at the place where the flange meets the neck.
4G9	The shell is used to shave off any excess clay from the base of the bottle, both to even up the shape and reduce weight.
4G10	Eventually the entire surface of the bottle will be gone over with the clam shell.
4G11	A smooth pebble is then used to compact the surface and leave a polish. The polishing should proceed as quickly as possible once the bottle is ready.
4G12	When the polishing is finished, it is time to compare with the original.

A BRIEF DESCRIPTION OF TRADITIONAL FIRING TECHNIQUES

By diligent practice in duplicating these various shapes it should be possible for you to replicate most of the ceramic forms you will encounter in the eastern two-thirds of North America. It is important to master each type before you go on to the next variety. In that manner you will be able to build on the skills you have learned. It is only with practice that you will be able to produce a technically and aesthetically satisfactory piece of work.

I will now discuss what is, in a way, the most important aspect of traditional ceramic technology: the actual firing of the finished pottery. This is a task that is both simple and difficult. I will briefly describe the process indicating those problems most likely to occur, speaking from my own experience.

Pottery must be absolutely dry before it is fired. If there is any moisture left in the clay, it will turn to steam and the pot will explode. At the first stage of drying, after you have finished construction and decoration work, the new vessel should be dried slowly. If possible, turn the pot upside down on its rim. This will slow the rate of drying and help to control warping. After the clay has turned a lighter color and no longer feels cool to the touch the drying can be speeded up. Modern Cherokee potters often speed up this final stage using the oven of a cooking stove.

Firing conditions are very important. There should be *no* wind. If, in the course of firing pottery, a cold draft should strike the red hot clay, the pot will crack. One of the advantages of the potter's kiln is that it can protect the hot ware from shattering drafts. In the simplest form of firing a shallow depression can be made in the ground, perhaps three feet in diameter. A wood fire is kindled in the center of this depression; be sure you have plenty of dry wood. If the wood is still green, it will burn slowly and will tend to pop a great deal as well as smoke heavily. If there is excessive popping, it can easily crack pottery.

When a nice fire with an ample bed of coals is ready, the dry pots can be pre-warmed around it. The traditional manner was to surround the fire with pots laid on their sides, with the rims facing inward. As the last bit of moisture is driven off, the clay will begin to change color. Pay careful attention to this process. The color change varies with the clays used, but you will be able to see clearly the change taking place. It will move from the edge of the rim downward along the sides toward the bottom. When the bottom, too, has changed color so that the pots show a uniform coloration, wait a few minutes.

The next step is one that must be done surely and deftly. Using a long stick, you must spread the sticks and coals of the heating fire about evenly in the middle of the depression. The pots are quickly rolled or lifted and placed on top of this bed of coals. The pots can be touching each other as well as stacked on top of each other. This must be done as quickly as possible. After the piling of the pottery is completed, the stack is covered with very dry wood. Small dead branches work very well. The pile of wood should be very ample to ensure that sufficient heat will be generated and to insulate the pottery against cold drafts. At this stage of the firing, you should not be able to see any of the pots inside the pile of wood. If you can, then pile on more branches until you can't see them. As the branches burn they will tend to collapse on the pile of pots. This process will develop a bed of incandescent coals that will gradually surround the pots. It is this bed of coals that will provide the source of heat that will fire the pottery. It is not the flames that will be shooting up in the air, taking the heat away. You must therefore pay careful attention to the buildup of a proper bed of coals. This is another reason why you must have a large supply of good dry material before beginning the firing process.

When, through the mass of burning coals, you can see the pots glowing red, the firing is completed. To produce a black ware the glowing mass of pottery and coals can be smothered with grass or rotten wood. Crushed corn cobs were traditionally used by Cherokee potters; buckets of saw dust are frequently used now. Sometimes potters will lift the glowing pots out of the fire with a stick, place them in a pit and then cover them with the crushed corncobs or saw dust. Pots that are not glowing but still hot enough to char organic material can be placed on their rims on top of a small pile of sawdust. The rim and interior will become a deep black that will contrast with the rest of the pot.

Cooking pottery was often swabbed with corn meal mush on the interior. It was felt that this process filled the pores of the clay better and produced a surface easier to clean.

If you want the clay to show primarily its natural color, the pottery should not be smothered. Sometimes dry grass can be thrown on the pile to burn. This will produce a light fluffy layer of ash that will help protect the hot pottery from drafts but will not produce a carbon build-up on the ware.

BIBLIOGRAPHY

Bell, Robert E. "Pottery Vessels from the Spiro Mound." *Oklahoma Anthropological Society Bulletin* 1 (1953): 25-38.

Dale, Vincent. "An Experiment in Ceramics." *Oklahoma Anthropological Society Bulletin* 22 (1973): 217-22.

Fewkes, V. J. "Catawba Pottery Making with Notes on Pamunkey Pottery Making, Cherokee Pottery Making and Coiling." *Papers of the American Philosophical Society* 88 (1944): 69-124.

Fontana, Bernard L. and others. *Papago Indian Pottery.* Seattle: University of Washington Press, 1962.

Fundaburk, Emma Lila, and Mary Douglass Fundaburk Foreman, eds. *Sun Circles and Human Hands: The Southeastern Indians Art and Industries.* Luverne, Ala.: 1957.

This work is an excellent source of illustrations from a number of out-of-print publications with a good bibliography. The best point of departure for any study of Southeastern culture.

Griffin, James B., ed. *Archaeology of Eastern United States.* Chicago: University of Chicago Press, 1952.

Guthe, Carl E. *Pueblo Pottery Making: A Study at the Village of San Ildefonso.* Papers of the Phillips Academy, Southwestern Expedition, no. 2. New Haven: Yale University Press, 1925.

Harrington, M. R. "Catawba Potters and Their Work." *American Anthropologist* 10 (1908): 399-407.

———. *The Last of the Iroquois Potters.* New York Museum Bulletin. Albany: 1909.

Holmes, William H. "Aboriginal Pottery of the Eastern United States." United States Bureau of American Ethnology. *Annual Report, 1898-1899.* Washington, D.C.: Government Printing Office, 1903.

The first extensive work on ceramics of this area. A great many illustrations. Much of the text is out of date.

MacNeish, Richard S. *Iroquois Pottery Types.* National Museum of Canada Bulletin no. 124. Anthropological Series no. 31. Ottawa: 1952.

Newman, Thomas M. "Documentary Sources on the Manufacture of Pottery by the Indians of the Central Plains and Middle Missouri." *Plains Anthropologist* 4 (1955): 13-20.

Shepard, Anna O. *Ceramics for the Archaeologist.* Carnegie Institution of Washington. Publication no. 609. Washington, D.C.: 1965.

MICHIGAN CHRISTIAN COLLEGE LIBRARY
ROCHESTER, MICH.

ENNIS AND NANCY HAM LIBRARY
ROCHESTER COLLEGE
800 WEST AVON ROAD
ROCHESTER HILLS, MI 48307